COMING IN HOT

IGNITING YOUR BRAND BEYOND THE LIMITS OF "GOOD ENOUGH"

BY JULIET WRIGHT

COMING IN HOT

To request permissions, contact the publisher at
publish@joapublishing.com or visit www.julietspeaks.com

Paperback ISBN: 978-1-961098-23-7
eBook ISBN: 978-1-961098-24-4
Printed in the USA.

Joan of Arc Publishing
Meridian, ID 83646
www.joapublishing.com

Table of Contents

Introduction

Welcome to the untamed world of branding: an uncharted territory made up of the ever-changing landscape of neighbors, marketing and advertising.

This combined space is as unpredictable as the Wild West itself.

Here, you'll find good guys masquerading as villains and villains cleverly concealing themselves as heroes.

There are no posted curfews to constrain the frenzy, no rulebook to guide you, and no etched boundaries to limit your ambitions. It's simply a dusty existence.

It's a realm where tumbleweeds carry whispers of sales, growth, and culture, all fueled by the moonshine of daring creative pioneers and strategic mavericks.

I have had enough of this chaos.

I'm not just blowing smoke. As the owner of a rapidly expanding branding agency that has guided over 250 companies to brand clarity, I've seen firsthand the monumental shift that intentional consistency makes.

A solid brand isn't something that materializes out of thin air; it's a masterpiece, meticulously crafted with vision, commitment, and purpose.

Today, I am not just a wanderer but the self-appointed sheriff of these lands, proudly pinning the badge onto my fierce red dress and letting the spurs jingle with every stride of my high heels.

I vow to wrangle clarity into this topic of branding once and for all.

I won't settle for mediocrity.

I'm here to push the boundaries, break free from convention, and carve my path.

I am determined to challenge the status quo and dismantle the smoke and mirrors with every step I take. For this illusion comes at the devastating price of more than just gold—the price is blood, sweat, and tears.

Blood and sweat may be a little harsh, but I am sure a collective river of innocent marketing interns' tears have been shed when sales quotas weren't met and fingers were pointed: a showdown that was over before it began.

We don't have to continue to survive in this way.

We have the power to replace the chaos with clarity, to add substance to the terms we throw around.

Let's blaze this trail with unwavering confidence, remembering only we hold the reins to our brands' futures.

CHAPTER ONE

Burn It Bright

Though my specialty lies in the domain of branding, the question I'm often asked is: what distinguishes branding from marketing and advertising?

The distinction isn't as intricate as you might imagine.

Think of these three—marketing, advertising, and branding—as components necessary for building a campfire.

I'm not talking about a pile of burning sticks. Anyone can make that. I'm talking about a real campfire, one with intention and personality. It's about creating a mesmerizing spectacle that draws oohs and aahs from onlookers—crafting a masterpiece that leaves a lasting impression.

A fire that can't help but draw in a community around it.

A crackling, warming, and hypnotic wonder, radiating a unique personality that captivates everyone who comes near.

While branding, marketing, and advertising are very different, all three are vital for radiating your product, service, or message out into the world. Each has a unique role to play and an order in which it is activated. It is the strategic handoff from one element to the next that will gain the cohesion, traction, and impact you are seeking.

May this image of the campfire clarify these three areas—a visual to hold onto and gather your team around. Bring the marshmallows. Let's go.

Branding: Building a Solid Foundation

The base must be solid and have your primary attention. Your brand is perfectly stacked dry logs—the must-haves that build your identity's backbone.

These logs represent essential elements like your values, mission, and promise to the world, along with your logo, fonts, colors, website, and business cards. They may seem ordinary on their own, but together, they create the essence of your brand—a collective mosaic of uniqueness and intention proclaiming, "Hello world, this is who we are!"

Every good fire foundation also has its fair share of kindling. On a campsite, kindling is made up of leaves, twigs, pinecones, and old newspapers. Alone, these elements seem insignificant and would burn out quickly, but kindling becomes instrumental in carrying the flame when paired with mighty logs.

Your sales toolkit, email signature, the background of your video call, and the clothes you wear to meetings all contribute to your kindling—the overall experience of your brand. The sum of these and hundreds of small details transforms your brand into a captivating identity.

A brand is built with both logs and kindling. Every company's assortment varies slightly. The lineup below provides a foundational start for a memorable brand. Pause and reflect on when you have dedicated attention to these elements. What needs to shift before you can move on?

Grab a pen and add a check (✔) next to the elements you feel need refined. Think of a deadline for addressing that element and write that date next to that element.

☐ Company's name

☐ Colors

☐ Logo

☐ Fonts

☐ Company apparel

☐ Voicemail message

☐ Company gifts

☐ Office decor

☐ Furniture

☐ Packaging

☐ Paper texture

☐ Pens

☐ Email signatures

☐ Vehicle wraps

☐ Hold music or messages

☐ Online chat appearance

☐ Physical space scent

☐ Employee onboarding materials

☐ Company swag

☐ Digital downloads or E-materials

☐ Social media filters and frames

☐ Profile and cover photos

☐ After-sales service experience

☐ Interactive elements

☐ Workspace or desk accessories

☐ Stamps or seals

☐ Receipt and invoice design

☐ Feedback forms

☐ Loyalty or reward cards

☐ Webinar and video graphics

☐ Presentation templates

☐ Mobile app interface and design

☐ Business reports and whitepaper designs

☐ Event booth design

☐ Name badges and lanyards

☐ User manuals or product guides

☐ Automated Email templates

☐ Podcast intro and outro

☐ Web browser icons and favicons

☐ Direct mail designs

☐ Newsletter layouts

☐ Client proposal templates

☐ Greeting cards

☐ Community outreach materials

This list is merely a starting point, yet it captures the essential elements crucial for building your brand.

With a solid foundation of branding in place, it's time to strike up your marketing.

Marketing: Setting the Fire Ablaze

Navigating the world of sales can be daunting and dark.

We've established that your brand is a carefully arranged stack of logs representing the core of your identity. But logs alone won't ignite a fire.

Enter marketing, your trusty match.

Marketing is the delicate art of crafting answers before your customers even think of the questions. Reading the minds of your customers is easier than you may realize; start with the classic five Ws: who, what, why, where, and when.

The precision of a "who" strikes against the rough surface of the market, creating a spark. The "what" and "why" boost this spark as they highlight the uniqueness of your purpose. That initial flame is all about positioning and promise.

The "where" and "when" determine the best conditions for lighting up. They guide your audience, ensuring they gather around your fire at the right time, preventing them from wandering aimlessly in the cold, dark night.

Without marketing, your brand—those carefully chosen logs—would sit cold, unnoticed and untouched in the vast forest of businesses. But the flame that marketing match ignites warms those nearby, drawing them closer, compelling them to stay and share stories.

Every "who, what, why, where, and when" in marketing ensures that your fire doesn't just start but keeps burning brightly, casting away shadows and uncertainties.

There is no shortage of questions that your potential clients, current customers, vendors, or ambassadors are asking. Below you will find a start—specific Ws to answer when you are aiming to develop your marketing strategy.

Who:

Who are the decision-makers in our target audience?

Who might be our most ardent supporters or advocates?

Who influences our target demographic?

What:

What sets our product or service apart from others?

What feedback have we received about our offerings?

What do customers frequently ask or complain about in our niche?

Where:

Where can we find communities or forums relevant to our offerings?

Where are the industry events or trade shows that we should attend?

Where are the gaps in the market that we can fill?

When:

When are the industry peak seasons or off-seasons?

When do we anticipate the next big trend or shift in the market?

When are our customers most active or receptive to marketing?

Why:

Why did we start this venture in the first place?

Why have similar ventures succeeded or failed?

Why would someone recommend our brand to a friend or colleague?

Let your marketing be the spark, the match, the catalyst into light.

When this slow burn is not enough, advertising is nearby, ready to show off its brilliance.

Advertising: The Fuel for the Flash

Imagine sitting by this campfire, logs neatly stacked, the steady fire from your marketing match flickering. But now you crave a brilliant burst of flames, an immediate, breathtaking glow.

That's where advertising comes into play, the lighter fluid to your fire.

We all want our fires to roar louder and shine brighter than the fires of those around us. That instant gratification, that immediate "oomph!"—advertising provides just that. It's the magic potion that can rapidly amplify your brand's visibility. Think of it as the blowhorn of those who have gone before, the secret map shortcut to the path that leads many directly to the warmth of your company's fire.

There is power in advertising.

The temptation is to jump to advertising before a solid foundation is built.

We've all heard those classic cautionary tales: eager businesses that drenched their brands in aggressive advertising campaigns in their haste for instant growth. But without a solid foundation, their flames grew wild, chaotic, and uncontrollable. Some merely singed their reputation, while others watched everything go up in smoke. With a thoughtful approach, advertising transforms a potential hazard into a brilliant asset.

With the right touch, advertising can turn your brand into a conversation starter, elevating your brand to legendary status—a huge success. This tool doesn't just foster quick connections or ignite powerful emotions; it solidifies your company among the elite, and in record time.

As we introduce this component to our campfire, exercise discernment. Like the masterful use of a secret ingredient, it's all about the right measure. Let advertising be the brilliant tool that harmonizes with the steady warmth of your branding and marketing, because true success lies in managing a flame that doesn't merely dazzle, but withstands time.

The spectrum of advertising opportunities is broad, and sometimes, commission incentives might influence the recommendations of sales representatives. It's crucial to consult a reputable advertising expert who can help you navigate the options and pinpoint what aligns best with your growth objectives. Here are just a few areas of advertising you may discuss with your advertising consultant:

Social media advertising

Influencer partnerships

Email marketing campaigns

Sponsored content

Video advertising

Outdoor advertising

Direct mail campaigns

Television commercials

Pay-per-click

Retargeting/remarketing

Radio and podcast advertising

Affiliate marketing

Display ads

Search engine marketing

Print ads

Product placement

Trade shows and exhibitions

Bringing It Together without Getting Burned

Running a branding agency is like being a pyromaniac—in the best way, of course.

Each dawn, we are not just sprinkling fairy dust; my team and I are conducting a symphony of sparks.

Setting the sky ablaze using a vivid palette of colors and designs.

Every so often, we get the opportunity to stand back and admire the roaring fire of our work, the warmth it brings to our client's heart and soul and the unexpected sparkle of confidence it brings the client—a pride they didn't know they desired in their core. With a sly grin and a casual nod, we soak in the radiant brilliance of a finished masterpiece, all while plotting our next creation.

Creative agencies are always chasing the next adventure: the bigger, the better. We are fueled by the adrenaline boost of turning the mundane into magnificent. This rush drives branding professionals to excel, always seeking to craft something extraordinary out of nothing.

This thrill is for you as well. Join me on this journey.

Starting today, vow to avoid falling into the trap of using branding, marketing, and advertising interchangeably, grasping randomly based on the day or budget. Instead, remember their roles in a well-built fire—each with its unique purpose and order.

Gather your logs with intention, kindle them with purpose, and ignite them with a well-struck match. And when the time is right, let that lighter fluid fly, propelling your company's brilliance into the hearts and minds of your audience.

When this concept is mastered, your company will be unstoppable.

Now, that's what it means to *Come In Hot*!

Reflect:

Which key insight from this chapter resonated most with you?

Share:

Who is someone who would benefit from this insight? List their name and consider reaching out to continue the conversation or share your thoughts.

Answer:

1. In which area—branding, marketing, or advertising—do you feel like you are excelling?

2. Which area—branding, marketing, or advertising—do you feel like you are overlooking the most?

3. What is your biggest obstacle preventing you from creating an impactful campfire for your business?

Analyze:

On a scale of excellence from "Ashamed" to "Invincible," how would you rate your current branding, marketing, and advertising efforts?

Branding

Ashamed | Unsure | Confident | Proud | Invincible

Marketing

Ashamed | Unsure | Confident | Proud | Invincible

Advertising

Ashamed | Unsure | Confident | Proud | Invincible

Action:

Categorize your current activities into the following areas: branding, marketing, and advertising.

CHAPTER TWO

Good Is Not Good Enough

We've all been there.

While walking out the door ten minutes late, your friend assures you that the stain on your shirt is "hardly noticeable."

In a desperate moment of online inspiration, your sister holds the scissors and insists that your hair will "grow out evenly."

You conjure your best fake smile as your sweet neighbor, who insisted on making your wedding cake "as a gift," says, "Sure, it leans a little to the left, but it will still taste great!"

Every scenario has a common theme: settling.

While the examples above are not life-changing, they do affect the confidence we carry in those situations. It is easy to move on by saying, "It's good enough."

"Good enough" is the line we tell ourselves far too often, especially in branding our company. This line is followed by a soft exhale of doubt.

We find ourselves drafting an excuse or lining up a lighthearted joke, just a little bridge taking up the room where complete confidence once stood. We step into situations with dreams of perfection, only to sometimes accept a smidge less sparkle than we'd hoped for. Whether the world sees and comments or looks the other way, our heart feels that tiny twinge of letdown.

There are several areas in our lives where we should never settle. Dating is definitely one of those.

Back in the days of dial-up internet, meeting your soulmate online was as likely as being hit by a lightning bolt while doing the moonwalk. Fast forward to today. Online dating has become the norm, responsible for more match-made-in-heaven stories than your neighborhood bar. As an alumni of the digital dating scene and someone who won the game by marrying the man I had directly messaged, I can vouch for the online dating appeal.

To fully grasp this tale, let's rewind to those days when I was a single mom of four with an early bedtime routine and a night that seemed endless and quiet. One evening, longing for adult conversation and resisting the urge to "accidentally" pocket-dial an ex-boyfriend for some chatter, I boldly ventured into the world of online dating.

The task seemed simple enough—set up a profile, which I naively estimated would be a few minutes of work. But oh, how wrong I was.

How do you condense thirty-two years of life, love, and everything in between into a 200-word bio and checkboxes? It felt like I was compressing my life's novel into a text message.

Just as I thought I had scaled the peaks of the bio challenge, ready for a moment of rest, the upcoming terrain of the photo section loomed. I needed merely six images to encapsulate every personality trait, hobby, and possible good side for my potential soulmate. I juggled between searching my memory-filled galleries and bravely turning my camera for fresh selfie endeavors.

I was determined not to settle, to work until the profile was complete. I carefully put in only my best.

After hours and hours invested in this profile, quitting wasn't an option. I finally closed my eyes, pushed submit, and my profile was live. My bio was charming, the pictures endearing, and my spirit was high. I didn't take the quick route. I didn't settle for just "good enough."

If we refuse to settle in our personal lives, why would we do so when building a brand?

Think about it: your brand is like your online dating profile—it needs to represent the best of you.

Your brand should communicate your unique essence and value to your potential "matches" in the market. First impressions matter. Whether it's that heart-fluttering first date or the crucial pitch to a potential client, there's no rewind button. It's a small golden window where opportunities are seized or missed.

A whipped-up, free logo or a mission statement scribbled in a hustle could be the silent culprits behind a polite "no, thank you" from potential clients.

When stakes are high, "good enough" should not be the standard. Whether you're in the vibrant quest for love or sculpting a brand identity, the goal should be nothing short of *absolutely remarkable*. After all, both you and your brand deserve nothing but the best.

Reflect:

Which key insight from this chapter resonated most with you?

Share:

Who is someone who would benefit from this insight? List their name and consider reaching out to continue the conversation or share your thoughts.

Answer:

1. In which aspects of your business do you find yourself compromising quality?

2. What elements are essential to you in forming a positive first impression?

3. Are there justifications you resort to when considering the shortcomings in your brand's presentation?

Analyze:

How often do you settle for "good enough" when making branding decisions?

Ashamed | Unsure | Confident | Proud | Invincible

Action:

Envision your company's branding as an online dating profile. Detail the unique qualities and standout features that would captivate your ideal "match."

CHAPTER THREE

The Sky Has Never Been the Limit

Every sale is multidimensional.

While you may be pitching to *one* individual, understand that often you are indirectly selling to an ensemble. No matter how adept you are at sales, the charisma of face-to-face interactions is only one component of closing a deal. After that initial "yes," the person you've impressed often takes up the role of a salesperson themselves, tasked with convincing their team, business partner, or spouse of the must-have product or service.

Recall the instances when you were ecstatic about an on-the-spot agreement with a potential client or customer, only to be met with silence later when you followed up. The contract that was meant to be signed remains untouched. Maybe it was buyer's remorse or perhaps cold feet, but if your digital footprint and physical branding tools aren't reflective of the vibrancy you personally bring, chances are, the sale fizzled out.

While this fade often happens out of sight, it is especially painful when it happens right in front of you.

Picture this: you board your flight and take your seat in first class. As the other passengers filter on, you engage in delightful banter with the person beside you. The two of you have so much in common, and you are able to easily name influencers in their industry. This is a dream, you think, a perfect fit for your company's new offering. Every word you exchange feels right; the universe conspired for this serendipitous meeting. You mentally calculate potential profits, smiling at the zeros trailing behind.

They are thinking the same thing. "It's like fate brought us together," they say. "What you sell is what I have been searching for." Just as you're about to toast to a new partnership, they pop the question: "What's your website? I'd love to share it with my business partner." Your heart sinks.

There you are, hoping that airplane mode shields you from the impending embarrassment. Because deep down, you're aware that your website isn't the gleaming, digital storefront it should be. It's closer to the opposite side of the spectrum. Outdated packages, an archaic design, and that headshot from a decade ago loom large. The once vibrant discussion of your company's avant-garde ethos grinds to an awkward halt. As they scroll and click yet another broken link, the enthusiasm dims. "Thanks," they mutter, reaching for their headphones.

The bottom line is clear: your brand assets need to echo the excellence you personally project. They should serve as seamless extensions of your personal image and charisma. Because you are selling to more than just one, having a congruent and updated brand presence isn't just good to have—it's nonnegotiable. Ensure your brand speaks as eloquently as you do, because sometimes, the silent language of visuals speaks louder than words.

Reflect:

Which key insight from this chapter resonated most with you?

Share:

Who is someone who would benefit from this insight? List their name and consider reaching out to continue the conversation or share your thoughts.

Answer:

1. How well do your brand assets back up the pitches your sales force make?

2. What feedback have you received about missing or ineffective sales tools?

3. Are there any elements of your brand representation that feel inauthentic or outdated?

Analyze:

Reflect on and rate the effectiveness and alignment of your sales materials and tools with your overall brand messaging.

Effectiveness

Disconnected | Inadequate | Aligned | Robust | Unbeatable

Alignment

Disconnected | Inadequate | Aligned | Robust | Unbeatable

Action:

Conduct a thorough review of all sales materials, ensuring each one authentically represents the brand, is up-to-date, and serves a functional purpose in the sales process.

CHAPTER FOUR

The "Weight" Is Over

Welcome to the heart of branding, where honesty reigns supreme.

You're on the wrong aisle if you are looking for a fairytale land of sugarcoated adventures. This chapter is where raw truth meets business, and authenticity isn't just a catchy phrase—it's the very core of our approach.

It's simple: branding thrives on genuine truths.

If you are feeling uneasy about facing some hard truths: deep breaths. I promise it will all be okay.

Imagine it's a new day and you've made the empowering choice to get healthier and more fit.

You're fired up and have just signed up with a personal trainer. In the first session, your brand-new shoes are laced, and your enthusiasm is high, but then comes the moment of truth—stepping onto the scale. The digital numbers staring back at you might feel like a jolt of reality, a chilly splash of water to your face. It's like you're walking the plank, where every step echoes with anticipation and anxiety.

The numbers staring back at you are more than just digits; they tell a story. They capture the moments you might've overlooked, the choices you've made.

You see an accumulation of time, perhaps months or even years of decisions, some attentive and others, perhaps, more neglectful. What was easy to hide is now illuminated by the gym's overhead lights.

But it's also the start—the honest foundation upon which all progress will be built.

It's the moment you face your current self, embrace your truths, and chart the path for the transformative journey ahead—the path where every drop of sweat, every disciplined choice, and every challenge you conquer will inch you closer to your goal.

In the world of branding, we don't deal with scales or body mass indexes, but the principles of honest assessment and setting clear, realistic goals remain the same.

You've got to strip your brand down to its skivvies, take a long hard look in the mirror, and assess the good, the bad, and the ugly.

I was once brought in for a branding "triage" consultation for a company that seemed to have hit a growth plateau. Their most glaring wound? Their logo. To say it had seen better days might be generous, assuming it had had any good days to begin with. We are talking about the equivalent of an '80s-aerobics-outfit outdated. It was a mystery as to who created or chose the logo in question.

Regardless of the Microsoft Paint enthusiast who had created the initial design, it desperately needed to be updated for the team to have confidence in their brand.

However, the real problem wasn't the logo's aesthetics. It was that the logo was the elephant in the room. Everyone on the leadership team despised it, but they kept their opinions silent in a well-meaning attempt to either spare feelings or not become the company outcast. The solution was simple: it was time for the team to face the truth.

I brought all the team members together and didn't waste time, cutting through the awkwardness like a hot knife through butter. Displaying the logo on the conference room screen, I took a deep breath and said, "This logo is terrible. It is an ugly, outdated front door keeping clients from your innovative and future-focused company."

Silence followed.

You could almost hear the collective heartbeats accelerating as each person braced for a potential wave of anger. But instead, the first audible sound was a sigh of relief, followed by genuine laughs and a room full of nods of agreement. The honesty was refreshing.

I was breaking down the walls of unnecessary politeness and hesitation, getting everyone on the same page.

In life, as in branding, we must face the facts and call a spade a spade. Only from this direct baseline of truth can we set meaningful goals and chart a course to success.

It's time to be brutally honest about your brand; your future success depends on it. So, step on that metaphorical scale, take a deep breath, and let's get to work. The "weight" is over!

Reflect:

Which key insight from this chapter resonated most with you?

Share:

Who is someone who would benefit from this insight? List their name and consider reaching out to continue the conversation or share your thoughts.

Answer:

1. In which facets of your brand do you find yourself sidestepping the raw truth?

2. What elements of your brand might you be hesitant to face, and why?

3. How might the avoidance of confronting these truths impact the growth and perception of your brand?

Analyze:

On a scale from "Veiled" to "Crystal Clear," where does your brand currently stand?

Veiled | Hazy | Diluted | Transparent | Crystal Clear

Action:

Conduct a "brand audit." Strip your brand bare and honestly evaluate its strengths and weaknesses. Highlight areas that shine and areas that require immediate attention. This exercise might be challenging, but it's the first step to genuine growth.

CHAPTER FIVE

Large Fries with a Side of Consistency

In branding, as in life, trust is the currency that pays the highest dividends.

Strip away all the frills—the catchy taglines and clever campaigns—and what you're left with is a simple fact: customers put their money, time, and loyalty into brands they trust.

Imagine yourself at the entrance of a McDonald's drive-through. Whether or not you're a fan of the fast-food giant, there's something undeniably magnetic about those towering Golden Arches. What is it? Trust. It's the very foundation upon which their empire has been built.

It's a trust that's as predictable as their french fries. Yes, I'm talking about the humble, crispy, golden strands of potato perfection. Whether you're five, fifteen, or eighty-five, you trust them to be just as you remember.

When you roll up to that drive-through and order a large fry, you're not just ordering food; you're tapping into a reservoir of trust built up since the first time you held a Happy Meal box in your tiny hands. There's a comforting predictability to it all. You know how they will taste, approximately how much it will cost, how many fries will be in that familiar red container, and you even know that a few extra fries will be scattered at the bottom of the bag. I call those the "bonus fries"—those bites you count on.

Building trust in a brand is similar to how we build trust in our relationships.

Think about those friendships you hold nearest and dearest to your heart. What makes you place such unwavering faith in them? More often than not, it's their steadfast reliability. Whether basking in the sunshine or caught in a storm, these friends stand by you, never faltering—consistently present, predictability there for you when you need them.

It creates an unbreakable bond of trust. It's not just about the big moments; it's about every little gesture, every reassurance that reminds you they've got your back.

Similarly, our relationships with companies or brands are built on trust formed through consistent experiences. In the bustling marketplace where choices are abundant, we naturally gravitate toward brands that offer a sense of familiar reliability. We depend on certain brands because they've proven, time and again, that they can deliver what they promise. When a brand consistently meets or even surpasses our expectations, our trust deepens. This repeated reliability—this unwavering commitment to quality and service—builds our loyalty.

Simply put, in the world of commerce, consistent excellence is the foundation of trust. Brands that understand and embody this are the ones we find ourselves returning to again and again. A solid brand doesn't just happen by accident. It results from careful planning, clear vision, unwavering commitment, and intentional consistency.

Intentional consistency means that every decision made—whether it's the colors chosen, the tone of a marketing campaign, or the after-sale follow-up service—is purposeful and aligned with the brand's core values. Every advertisement, every product launch, and every customer interaction is a testament to the brand's promise.

It's not just about doing things the same way every time, but doing them with a clear understanding of the "why" behind each action.

When a brand is consistently true to its values, it sends a powerful message.

Like the friend who always keeps their word, who's always there for you, whose actions align with their promises, the trust you place in a brand isn't built overnight but is an accumulation of all the consistent, reliable experiences you've had. Being that brand is about living up to that image, time and time again. Through this deliberate consistency, a brand doesn't just sell products or services; it builds trust, fostering a bond with its customers that's hard to break.

While products might attract customers, it's trust that retains them. To be more than just a name in the market, remember: be consistent, be intentional, and let the trust you build be the cornerstone of your brand's legacy.

To truly thrive, your brand needs to be like those McDonald's fries—a consistent experience that delights and meets expectations time after time. If you can establish that level of trust, you've already won half the branding battle.

Reflect:

Which key insight from this chapter resonated most with you?

Share:

Who is someone who would benefit from this insight? List their name and consider reaching out to continue the conversation or share your thoughts.

Answer:

1. Reflect on a time you felt betrayed or let down by a brand. What led to this sentiment?

2. What aspects of your brand consistently evoke trust from your clients or customers?

3. Are there moments when your brand has diverged from its core values? How did you or would you address this?

Analyze:

On a trustworthiness scale, where do you think your clients would rate your brand?

Betrayed | Hesitant | Dependable | Loyal | Unbreakable

Action:

Identify an area of your business that needs strengthening in terms of consistency. Develop a strategic plan over the next month to improve and standardize this aspect, ensuring it aligns with your brand values.

CHAPTER SIX

Dreams to Delivery

Starting something new is daunting. No matter the scale or scope, taking that initial step often feels like staring into the vast unknown. There are always reasons to postpone the plunge: "I'm not ready yet," "What if it fails?" or the most common, "Maybe someday." The fear of the unknown, the dread of judgment, and the overwhelming sense of responsibility can be paralyzing.

Every budding entrepreneur faces a moment—a moment where the vastness of their aspirations meets the uncertainty of reality.

Yet, every brand you admire, every business you frequent, every entrepreneur you respect—all began with a single step. They started with an idea, a dream, and the audacity to believe in their vision, no matter how distant it seemed.

Many of my clients had been holding onto their dreams for years, some hidden away as tight as a secret, some living in conversations of what ifs, all waiting for the perfect moment. But here's a little tip: there is no perfect moment. There's only the moment you decide to take charge and make your dream a reality.

I had one remarkable client who I still think of today. She had dedicated her life to human resources—always behind the scenes, orchestrating for others, working for larger corporations. However, within her heart was a blossoming dream to venture out on her own to craft a unique niche in HR, offering invaluable consulting, transformative workshops, and personalized coaching: a vision that would empower individuals and teams to soar higher than they ever imagined.

Years passed, and this dream was like a melody she couldn't shake off, continually humming in the background of her day-to-day. The transition from a steady job to the unpredictable world of entrepreneurship is never easy. But when she took that leap, our paths crossed, and I got to play a part in her entrepreneurial journey.

I remember the day she saw her logo for the first time. It wasn't just ink on paper or pixels on a screen; it was the embodiment of years of passion, ambition, and tenacity. The emotion in her eyes and the pride in her stance were evident. And as she flipped through her new branded folder, scribbled with her pen, explored her sales page, admired her promotional video, glanced at her professional portrait, handed out her business card, and navigated her website—each bearing her unique logo and colors—there was a transformative air around her. No longer just an HR professional, she now bore the proud title of "Owner."

But it didn't stop there. The real joy came when she shared her brand with her extended family. Their initial assumption was that she had bought into a well-established franchise. But her radiant smile grew even brighter as she declared that she wasn't just a *part* of this brand—she was its founder. The company was her own creation.

As a natural entrepreneur myself, moments like these reaffirm why I do what I do. The sheer joy of turning intangible dreams into tangible realities is unmatched. I often think about parents in the delivery room, holding their newborn for the first time, feeling a world of emotions as they gaze upon that tiny face. While I would never *equate* the profound miracle of life to the inception of a business—the exhilaration, the sense of achievement, the euphoria—there are undeniable parallels. And in those moments, witnessing the birth of a brand, the world feels just a bit brighter.

But remember, creating a brand doesn't mean you have to wear all the hats. The most successful ventures often aren't solo endeavors. They're collaborations, a coming together of minds, skills, and passions. Just as a village raises a child, a community builds a brand. There are experts, like brand designers, consultants, and strategists, who dedicate their lives to helping bring visions to life. You don't have to be an expert in every field. That's what teams are for.

Allow yourself the luxury of dreaming without bounds, then find those who can help transform those dreams into reality. Your brand doesn't have to exist solely in your imagination or as scribbles in a notebook. It can breathe, evolve, and inspire—but only if you take that first step.

Today is the day. It's time to watch your brand come to life. Every great journey begins with a single, brave step. You are ready.

Reflect:

Which key insight from this chapter resonated most with you?

Share:

Who is someone who would benefit from this insight? List their name and consider reaching out to continue the conversation or share your thoughts.

Answer:

1. Which personal aspiration or dream has been persistent in your thoughts?

2. What's the biggest fear you need to overcome to take the next step?

3. Who in your network has the skills or experience to help bring your idea to life?

Analyze:

Reflect on and rate your level of clarity, confidence, and readiness to bring your dream to life.

Clarity
Uncharted | Developing | Formed | Dedicated | Fearless

Confidence
Uncharted | Developing | Formed | Dedicated | Fearless

Readiness
Uncharted | Developing | Formed | Dedicated | Fearless

Action:

Mark your calendar with a specific date, three months from today, as your "Dream Forward Day." By this date, commit to taking tangible steps, no matter how small, toward realizing your dream. Whether it's registering a business name, designing a logo, or simply booking a consultation with an expert, ensure that this deadline propels you into action toward your vision.

CHAPTER SEVEN

Facing Your Midlife Branding Crisis

The classic identity crisis isn't just a rite of passage for reckless teens or those in a crazy midlife quest, all in the name of finding purpose.

Just like individuals, companies can also find themselves navigating the dilemma of an identity crisis.

Indeed, the struggle is real.

One clear method for assessing the strength of your brand identity is to imagine it as a person. Imagine your brand enters a bustling networking event filled with prospective clients and competitors. Everyone is sipping their cocktails and engaging in small talk. There's a chorus of conversations, the buzz of business deals sealing, and connections taking root.

Does your brand stride confidently into the crowd?

Do people pause mid-conversation, heads turn, and widen? Does your brand command attention—not beca it's the loudest or the most flashy, but because it carries its with a quiet confidence that can't be ignored.

Can you describe your brand in just three words?

If you can, chances are you've built a strong brand identity.

If you're struggling to find those words, don't worry—you're not alone. Many businesses find themselves in a perpetual cycle of identity confusion or crisis.

In today's hyperconnected age, word-of-mouth marketing remains one of the most influential and organic ways for brands to grow. Yet, it presents an intriguing problem. While businesses heavily rely on their customers to sing praises and spread the good word, many companies need to improve on giving those customers a clear message to share. It's the challenge of wanting someone to pass on a secret but not telling them what that secret is.

As Jeff Bezos, the founder of Amazon, has been widely quoted as saying, "Your brand is what other people say about you when you're not in the room."

So, what do you want them to say? If you're struggling to answer that, then you've found the heart of the issue. How can you expect your customers to be brand ambassadors if you don't even know the message they're supposed to champion?

Branding is articulating this identity with clarity, ensuring every stakeholder, from your top leaders to your customers, understands and resonates with it. Only then can word-of-mouth marketing truly work its magic, echoing a brand's true message far and wide.

Let's take a moment for deep reflection. Dive into the heart of your brand.

Are you the quirky startup shaking up the industry with innovative solutions? Or are you the trusted legacy brand clients turn to for unmatched quality and reliability? Are you the daring maverick who challenges the status quo, or the empathetic listener who always puts customers first? Once you have a clear grasp of who you are, the world around you will start to see it too.

When people talk about your brand, they are likely to use the same phrases over and over. Are you proud of the words they repeat?

Once those phrases become linked with your brand they appear everywhere—in warm introductions, online reviews, and referrals—building a powerful, self-perpetuating cycle of recognition and trust.

When you're confident in your brand's identity, it trickles down to every aspect of your business. Your marketing becomes more focused, your messaging more consistent, your advertising more targeted, and your customer interactions more authentic. It's so real that in the eyes of your audience, your brand becomes less of a faceless corporation and more of a familiar friend. In a world saturated with brands fighting for our short attention spans, a strong identity isn't just a bonus—it's a must-have.

Your brand's identity is what sets it apart from the crowd.

Embrace it, celebrate it, and let it shine through in everything you do. And that's how you turn an identity crisis into an identity triumph.

If your brand's identity is foggy, simply take it as an opportunity for a makeover—a chance to look in the mirror, adjust your tie or fix your makeup, and stride back out there with newfound confidence. Because when your brand knows exactly who it is, the world will know it too.

Reflect:

Which key insight from this chapter resonated most with you?

Share:

Who is someone who would benefit from this insight? List their name and consider reaching out to continue the conversation or share your thoughts.

Answer:

1. If your brand was a person, how would it introduce itself at a social gathering?

2. What emotions or impressions do you believe customers currently associate with your brand?

3. How would you want a loyal customer to describe your brand to a friend?

Analyze:

On a scale from "Lost" to "Unshakable," how would you rate your brand's current sense of identity?

Lost | Searching | Discovering | Defined | Unshakable

Action:

Write down three core values you want your brand to represent. Reflect on whether your current strategies and messaging align with these values.

CHAPTER EIGHT
The Rhythm of a Reputation

As the familiar saying goes, change is the only constant in life. Change is evident in every area of our lives. In business, we observe shifts in products, prices, staff, locations, and even the essence of our brand.

Humans are naturally creatures of habit, often seeking comfort from what we know. When confronted with change, our first instinct can be resistance or suspicion.

A colleague moves to a new city, and chatter hints at financial troubles. The team lead is promoted into a new role, yet in the breakroom, uninformed coworkers speak in hushed tones as they insinuate that performance issues must have been what "forced" the move. A relationship concludes and before sunset, whispers spread, suggesting a sensational story behind a scandal.

More often than not, the reasons behind changes are positive and far less dramatic than we imagine.

Brands are no exception. A shift in branding typically indicates an exciting evolution, but communication is critical for keeping alarm bells from sounding.

Just as in a ballroom dance, where the leader sets the direction and pace, businesses must take the lead in the narrative surrounding their transformation. By doing so, they can ensure that stakeholders move harmoniously rather than stepping on toes or moving out of sync.

An effective brand should encapsulate the essence of your business. While there's no definitive rule for when a company should update its brand, specific indicators suggest a potential need for a refresh. These indicators include experiencing significant growth, entering new markets, undergoing industry shifts, or finding that your brand no longer resonates with its mission, values, or target demographic.

If you're hesitant about your brand or feel less enthusiastic about showcasing it, maybe it's becoming outdated or losing its relevance.

A visual or strategic brand update will reinvigorate the company's image and signal to stakeholders that the company is evolving, adapting, and poised for future success.

Much like a caterpillar's metamorphosis into a butterfly, signaling growth and maturity from humble beginnings, a well-orchestrated brand change can surprise and captivate those unaware of its transformative potential.

While updating a company's logo, color palette, font, or overall aesthetic may seem straightforward, the crucial component is guiding the dialogue surrounding this change, emphasizing all positive aspects of growth. If not managed proactively, this narrative can lead to misconceptions and misunderstandings.

Leading such conversations builds more than just understanding; it solidifies trust. In today's dynamic business landscape, transparency isn't just a buzzword; it's the lifeblood of enduring relationships.

When informed, stakeholders rally behind the company, appreciating the vision behind these changes and recognizing their strategic importance for sustainable growth. To sum it up, as businesses tread the evolutionary path, their route should be clear, transparent communication, ensuring not only a smoother transition but the unwavering support of their most valued allies.

After all, when it comes to the rhythm of business and brand reputation, it's always wiser to set the tempo than to scramble to someone else's beat.

Reflect:

Which key insight from this chapter resonated most with you?

Share:

Who is someone who would benefit from this insight? List their name and consider reaching out to continue the conversation or share your thoughts.

Answer:

1. How has your company evolved or expanded lately?

2. How do you currently gauge the perception of your brand during times of transition or change?

3. What proactive measures have you taken to ensure stakeholders understand and support the reasons behind your brand's changes?

Analyze:

Evaluate how adeptly your brand navigates and conveys its transitions. Using the following scale, determine your brand's *agility* when faced with change.

Resistant | Unprepared | Adapting | Leading | Masterful

Action:

Draft a communication blueprint for your next brand change, ensuring it highlights the positive aspects of growth and evolution.

CHAPTER NINE

Communication Dialed In

A brand is a living, breathing entity that thrives on clear, consistent communication.

It's more than how your brand talks to its customers—it's also about how it communicates internally, from the top leadership all the way to the new intern who just started.

Picture the innocent game of telephone, a staple of childhood gatherings and playful parties. A line of eager participants wait in anticipation. The first person, entrusted with creating the original message, whispers it carefully to the next. As the message travels from ear to ear, through a chain of giggles and misinterpretations, its integrity is tested. By the time the last person in the line stands to announce the "message" they received, what's revealed is often a comically muddled version of the initial statement. From the start to the end, this transformation is usually met with laughter and sometimes disbelief at just how far from the source it has strayed.

Transport this scene from a child's birthday party to a bustling corporate office. Replace the giggling kids with department heads, team leads, and junior executives. The whispered message is no longer a harmless secret; it's your brand's vision, mission statement, or the rebrand strategy for the upcoming quarter. The consequence of misinterpretation or dilution in this setting isn't a round of chuckles but could more likely be a cascade of misaligned actions, confused employees, and, potentially, misguided decisions.

In a game setting, the distortion is the fun part; it's expected. In a business environment, especially regarding brand communication, distortion isn't just unexpected—it's detrimental. The game of telephone becomes a metaphor for the challenges of maintaining clear and consistent communication within an organization. The stakes are higher, and the consequences of a "distorted message" are far-reaching, affecting brand integrity, employee morale, and, potentially, the company's bottom line.

Communication must start from the top and filter through each level before arriving to the customer. While customers are the ones spending the money, your loyalty and transparency is owed to your staff first.

Have you ever been to a restaurant and, walking to the front door, spot an intriguing special of the day on the chalkboard? You stride in, confident about your choice even before you're handed a menu.

"I'll have the special," you tell the server, who gives you a blank stare.

She doesn't know what the special is. Your excitement deflates, and in a moment, you are frustrated, and she is embarrassed. You both smile politely and move on like it is no big deal, but the damage has been done.

The message about the special started at management and missed a crucial step: communicating it to the staff.

It went directly to the customers. This disconnect creates an awkward situation and leaves the server feeling like she isn't a valuable part of the team and the customer questioning their own willingness to stay.

Brand communication must *begin* at the top and *not stop* at the top.

The executive team must understand and support a brand's vision and identity *before* that vision and identity trickle down through other leadership to management and on to frontline staff. Only then can it be effectively communicated to vendors, partners, and, ultimately, customers.

Every member of your organization has invested time and energy into your company. They deserve to be informed and included in the brand communication process. Remember, tiny cracks at the top can quickly turn into gaping canyons at the bottom.

It's vital that everyone in your organization not only knows what your brand stands for but can also articulate it confidently and consistently. This way, you ensure that your brand's identity stays intact no matter how often it's communicated.

It's time to break the telephone game pattern. Let's take whispers that get distorted down the line and articulate them clearly to turn them into rallying cries, meetings, and memos that inspire and motivate everyone in your organization. Let's make sure the message remains consistent from the top down and from the inside out. This way, everyone in the organization becomes a brand ambassador, reinforcing your brand's identity with each internal and external interaction.

With consistent, clear communication, every member of your organization will know your brand as well as they know themselves. And that's a win for everyone.

Reflect:

Which key insight from this chapter resonated most with you?

Share:

Who is someone who would benefit from this insight? List their name and consider reaching out to continue the conversation or share your thoughts.

Answer:

1. When was the last time you experienced a breakdown in internal brand communication?

2. How often do you check in with different levels of your organization to ensure they understand the brand message?

3. Are your frontline employees as equipped to communicate the brand message as your top executives?

Analyze:

On a scale from "Muddled" to "Seamless," how would you describe the clarity and consistency of your brand's internal communication?

Clarity

Muddled | Fragmented | Clarifying | Synchronized | Seamless

Consistency

Muddled | Fragmented | Clarifying | Synchronized | Seamless

Action:

Organize a brand communication workshop for all levels of your organization to ensure everyone is confident in delivering an elevator pitch about your company.

CHAPTER TEN
Craft the Canvas

You've likely experienced that moment of uncertainty when you can't pinpoint exactly what you're looking for until it's right in front of you.

Similarly, in the world of branding, it's often hard to articulate or visualize what our brand needs until an expert brings clarity. This is why engaging a professional in the branding process is so crucial.

These professionals don't just see the surface; they dive deep. They have a gift for drawing out nuances from your stories, understanding your passions, catching that animated tone in your voice or particular sparkle in your eye when you discuss what you love. While these aspects might not seem directly linked to branding at first glance, they are windows into the unique personality and charm your brand needs.

Is your look sleek and glossy, or raw and matte? Does it channel modern sophistication, or resonate with vintage charm? Is it complex and intricate, or refreshingly simple?

Dining at a five-star restaurant is an experience unlike any other. While they might use the same ingredients we find in our local grocery store or farmers market, these top chefs craft dishes in imaginative ways we wouldn't think of.

Their talent lies in blending flavors, creating meals that often surprise our taste buds. When we step into such establishments, it's not just the enticing menu that captures our attention but also the artfully presented dishes at neighboring tables. It's a reminder that sometimes, the best experiences are those that go beyond our usual expectations, introducing us to flavors and combinations we didn't even know we'd love.

Like a favorite meal, crafting your brand's identity is a sensory journey.

Engaging all five senses is paramount; you should be able to visualize, touch, hear, smell, and even taste elements of your brand. This detailed approach paves the way for an authentic brand identity.

Sight is arguably the most influential sense when it comes to branding since visual elements define the immediate impressions and connections people make with your brand. Colors, shapes, and typography aren't just aesthetic choices; they carry subconscious messages. A sleek, minimalist design might convey efficiency and modernity, while a rustic, hand-drawn logo might evoke feelings of nostalgia and authenticity. Every visual detail—from your logo to the layout of your website, the imagery you use in campaigns, and even your staff's attire—should paint a coherent picture of your brand's style and values.

Equally important as harnessing sight is engaging touch. In an increasingly digital age, the feel of the tangible aspects of your brand become even more valuable. The texture of the paper you use for brochures, the weight and feel of your product in a customer's hand, or the plush comfort of a waiting area in your office can all communicate aspects of your brand. Is your product packaging rough and eco-friendly, hinting at sustainable values? Or is it sleek and glossy, suggesting luxury? In events or physical spaces associated with your brand, even the ambient temperature and the materials of surfaces—smooth marble counters or rustic wooden benches—all resonate on a tactile level, further deepening the sensory connection someone has with your brand.

Now think about the characteristic sounds associated with your brand. Does your brand or company have a jingle or a signature tone that plays during advertisements? The ambiance in your store or at your events has a sound—maybe the murmur of conversation, soft background music, or the hum of machinery. For tech brands, the subtle sounds their devices make when receiving notifications or being turned on can be crucial acoustic brand markers. The cadence, tone, and pitch of how your representatives speak also play into auditory branding. When customers hear these sounds, they should instantly recall the spirit of your brand.

Did you know that scents evoke strong emotions and memories? Whether or not you have included them intentionally, scents are a robust component of your brand. Some retail stores have instantly recognizable signature scents that waft out whenever you pass by. Car manufacturers often invest in creating a particular "new car" scent. If your brand was a scent, what would it be? Freshly baked bread? A hint of citrus? The musk of leather? Whether you utilize the sense of smell through product scents, environmental aromas, or even the smell of the paper or materials used in packaging, ensure it resonates with what your brand stands for.

The sense of taste is obvious for brands directly dealing with food and beverages. But even outside that sphere, taste can play a role. If you were to host an event or a product launch, what kind of refreshments would align with your brand? Bold, spicy flavors denote innovation and risk-taking, while classic, well-loved recipes signify trustworthiness and tradition. Even the quality of beverages and appetizers at an event communicate a brand's standards and attention to detail.

By intertwining these sensory elements, you achieve more than recognition. An intentional blend crafts a memorable, holistic experience that audiences don't just observe, but deeply feel.

Your brand's imagery is not just a single image; rather, it encompasses a vast playground. From photographs to drawings, details, landscapes, shapes, symbols, and expressions—they all have a place. One powerful way to encompass all of the senses in one place is by creating a mood board. Whether mounted on a wall or taped to a notebook page, a tangible mood board is a unified tapestry of these visuals that defines your style.

Your mood board becomes a window into this cohesive vision, a beautiful mosaic of elements that represents your brand. The end result should resonate with you, providing a representation of a brand you are immensely proud to call your own.

Building a brand is a thoughtful, exploratory process, one that starts with understanding the depth of your own vision and then giving it a form, a voice, a presence.

Reflect:

Which key insight from this chapter resonated most with you?

Share:

Who is someone who would benefit from this insight? List their name and consider reaching out to continue the conversation or share your thoughts.

Answer:

1. Which emotions are elicited by your current brand's visual aesthetics?

2. In terms of texture and feel, which material best represents your brand?

3. If your brand were to be captured in a scent, what would it resemble?

Analyze:

Reflect on the *depth* of your brand's sensory identity and rate it below.

Fragmented | Emerging | Defined | Robust | Ultimate

Action:

To achieve a holistic identity, design a sensory mood board for your brand, encompassing visuals, touch, sound, scent, and taste.

CHAPTER ELEVEN

Empower Each Element

Imagine this: You're in the midst of the hiring process, you know exactly what position you need filled, and you want your potential applicants to know it too.

You work diligently, crafting a job description to outline the role's responsibilities, qualifications, and expectations. You know a well-defined job description is crucial to finding the right fit.

Why then do we neglect to do the same for the branding elements we create?

Think of your branding elements—your logo, website, marketing collateral—as team members. They each have a unique role to perform.

In the haste of creation it's tempting to gloss over a simple question that could change the game—what is each element's job?

Have you ever paused to consider these crucial questions?

What is your logo's job?

The job of your logo could act as a guiding light at a busy intersection, a bold sign drawing attention to your brick-and-mortar location. Or your logo's job might solely grace the digital realm, delicately stamping its presence on your online store. Both jobs are vital yet distinct and could affect the overall design choices, colors, and fonts.

What is your website's job?

A website might serve as an external magnet to attract new clients, a collective tool box of information for existing customers, or a net for potential leads. Or the job of your website may be strictly internal: a platform to entice top-tier talent, potentially influencing their decision to join your company. For your current employees, your website may hold space as a proud showcase of the company they belong to, playing a role in staff retention. While each function might be subtle, they are embedded within the website's design, content, and the strategic placement of call-to-action buttons.

We all know that sales are crucial, but not every branding element needs to focus on sales. Remember that time you said, "I've got sales covered. What I really need is . . ."? Once you're clear on what that job is, you're halfway there. You wouldn't hire someone without clarity on their role, expecting them to just figure it all out, would you? Yet, we often leave our branding elements to fend for themselves.

The next time you're about to create a branded piece, hit the pause button. Ask, "What is its job?" Write its "job description." This simple exercise can make your branding elements more efficient and, by extension, your brand more potent.

To better understand this, let's dive into the process.

The first step is to evaluate the effectiveness of each branding element.

Imagine you're a manager conducting an annual performance review. Ask yourself, "Is my logo fulfilling its purpose? Is the website up to par? Would I 'hire' that piece again as it is now?" You may discover that, just like employees, some branding elements need a little more coaching (revising), or in extreme cases, you might need to let them go. Regular checks help identify gaps and potential improvements.

Next, ensure the needs are constant throughout. In this step, consistency is crucial. Just as a well-orchestrated team rallies around a unified message, your branding elements, despite their different roles, should communicate cohesively. If your sales team started pitching a product that contradicted your company's values, you would step in immediately. Likewise, your branding elements must align with your brand's core message.

As you develop "job descriptions" for your branding elements, you'll find that these descriptions also make excellent creative briefs for your design team. This clarity can guide the design process, ensuring that the final product ticks all the boxes.

Effective branding isn't solely the responsibility of your marketing department. It's a team effort.

Step three is to intentionally plan a company-wide meeting where everyone from customer service to IT understands the "jobs" of your branding elements. This shared understanding can lead to greater cohesion, authenticity, and overall brand success.

Finally, just as your team evolves, gaining new skills and achieving new milestones, so should your branding elements develop. Update their "job descriptions" to reflect shifts in your business goals, the market trends, or customer expectations.

By paying attention to these aspects, you're setting your brand up for success. Writing a "job description" may be the simple step you're missing that will make a world of difference in crafting a stronger, more consistent, and ultimately, more successful brand.

Reflect:

Which key insight from this chapter resonated most with you?

Share:

Who is someone who would benefit from this insight? List their name and consider reaching out to continue the conversation or share your thoughts.

Answer:

1. Which team members are essential for understanding and implementing branding decisions?

2. How frequently do you assess the performance of your branding elements?

3. Which branding components are currently absent or underutilized in your strategy?

Analyze:

Evaluate your current approach to defining and utilizing your branding elements and rate it on the scale below.

Defining
Inactive | Inconsistent | Developing **|** Streamlined | Perfected

Utilizing
Inactive | Inconsistent | Developing **|** Streamlined | Perfected

Action:

Draft a detailed job description for your primary branding asset, ensuring it aligns with your company's overarching goals.

CHAPTER TWELVE

Battle-Ready Branding

Have you ever embarked on a do-it-yourself project that seemed straightforward online, only to discover that critical components or tools were nowhere to be found?

You were confident you could wrap it up before lunch, but suddenly your project morphed into a frustrating day with the printer out of ink, the leftover paint dried up, and the search for tools that has taken you far beyond the garage. The day wraps up with not one, not two, but three trips to the hardware store. A day like this can make the best of us swear off projects for years to come.

Such experiences are not uncommon in the realm of branding when organizations lack preparation. While they include fewer wood shavings and power tools, they can be equally frustrating.

Picture this: you are invited to appear on a wildly popular podcast. It's a dream come true. All the hosts request is your professional headshot, a bio, and a transparent version of your logo. This task appears simple until you realize your headshot is no longer on your desktop, your bio needs to be updated, and the only version of your logo is in your old colors and the completely wrong format.

What initially seemed like an exciting opportunity now resembles an annoying scavenger hunt for missing brand elements. Clients and other important work get pushed to the back burner. You know this opportunity will not come again.

It's crucial for every company to prepare a "brand arsenal" to avoid such predicaments. This comprehensive, well-organized, and readily accessible collection should encompass all your branding materials: logos, images, videos, links, summaries, intros, infographics, sales pieces, case studies, press release templates, and portfolio pieces.

Keeping these materials updated and ready to deploy at a moment's notice can save considerable time and effort and avoid unnecessary frustration.

In the moment of need, it may feel like it is all about convenience, but a brand arsenal extends beyond; it is about preserving your brand's integrity.

There's a temptation to recreate or hastily edit existing brand elements under looming deadlines or high-pressure demands. However, each unauthorized edit or re-creation threatens the consistency and integrity of your brand. Over time, slight alterations can accumulate, leading to an inconsistent brand image that confuses your audience and dilutes your brand's power.

Suppose a nonprofit banquet you are sponsoring needs your logo, but you can't provide it promptly. In that case, they might resort to using a low-resolution version from your website, resulting in a distorted representation of your brand. Suddenly, the large amount you paid as a sponsor feels like it may have contributed to hurting your reputation rather than helping it.

Brand guidelines are essential and act as the definitive playbook for your brand's visual identity, meticulously detailing the correct usage of logos, colors, fonts, and more.

When collaborating with partners for co-branding initiatives, these guidelines clarify how your brand should be showcased. Brand guidelines are pivotal at every touchpoint where your brand interacts with the world, thickening its identity and ensuring it remains memorable.

Every brand has a unique personality and story, which must be reflected consistently across all channels in your communication style, content, and visuals. The importance of employee training must not be understated. Each team member needs to understand and adhere to your brand guidelines, further solidifying brand integrity and improving customer experience.

The brand arsenal should evolve with your brand. Whether adding new assets, removing outdated ones, or updating existing ones, your assets should accurately represent your brand at any given point. Thankfully, advancements in technology have made managing brand tool kits easier. Digital asset management tools streamline storing, updating, and sharing your brand assets, reducing the risk of inconsistencies.

Someone in your organization or professional agency will need to be on watch, conducting regular brand audits. These audits are a fundamental part of this process, ensuring that your brand elements are used correctly and your brand's image remains consistent across all platforms.

By ensuring that your ecosystem of elements is readily available, well-managed, and consistently applied, you safeguard your brand's identity, making every marketing effort more effective.

Brands can learn invaluable insights from case studies of other brands that have either excelled in maintaining a consistent brand image or faced challenges due to inconsistencies. These real-world examples guide you on the dos and don'ts of brand management, providing precious lessons on preserving your brand's integrity. To find a case study that relates to your particular brand's needs, simply do an online search for "brand case study: ____" with your company's niche or branding need in the space. For instance, if you are in the restaurant business, you could search, "brand case study: restaurant." Or if you are in need of a new logo, you could search, "brand case study: updated logo."

Don't scramble for the necessary brand elements when the next opportunity presents itself. Instead, be ready to seize the moment, confident in your brand's consistent, compelling representation.

Reflect:

Which key insight from this chapter resonated most with you?

Share:

Who is someone who would benefit from this insight? List their name and consider reaching out to continue the conversation or share your thoughts.

Answer:

1. How organized and accessible are your current brand assets?

2. Which of your branding materials require immediate updates or revisions?

3. How well-equipped is your team in maintaining and representing the brand's integrity?

Analyze:

Reflect on the consistency, accessibility, and current state of your brand elements and rate them below.

Consistency of brand elements

Neglected | Inconsistent | Streamlined | Refined | Impeccable

Accessibility of brand elements

Neglected | Inconsistent | Streamlined | Refined | Impeccable

Current state of brand elements

Neglected | Inconsistent | Streamlined | Refined | Impeccable

Action:

Initiate a comprehensive review and inventory of your brand elements to ensure cohesion and readiness.

CONCLUSION
A Challenge and an Invitation

In the ever-evolving world of business and branding, the greatest companies don't just show up; they make an entrance.

They come in hot.

Each company stewards a blazing fire that doesn't fade, not even in the darkest nights: a fire built on the solid foundation of branding, lit by marketing, and accelerated by advertising.

Refusing to settle for mediocrity, these companies push boundaries and continually strive for more.

As we've traversed this journey together, it's clear that your brand isn't merely a logo, a color, or a font. It's an embodiment of values, vision, and purpose. It's your company's battle cry and its softest whisper.

We've explored the crucial role of trust, dived into the complexities of perception, and discovered the power of transparent communication. We've also weighed the fine line between brand evolution and maintaining consistency.

Coming in hot isn't about blind acceleration.

It's about intentional, well-guided momentum.

More than anything, it's about recognizing that "good enough" is neither good nor enough.

Fill up with the fuel of passion to surpass the ordinary.

This is a challenge, and an invitation.

Branding ensures that every interaction—whether in-person or digital—and each impression is delivered with purpose and intent.

Branding is being the beacon in a saturated market, leading rather than being led.

As you close this book, remember this: Branding isn't a one-off task but an ongoing journey.

It's a commitment to never settle, to push boundaries, and to light up the business realm with a brilliance that's uniquely yours.

A Challenge and an Invitation

The stage is set. Ignite your brand, elevate its essence, and transcend the limits of the ordinary.

The world is waiting.

About The Author:

Juliet Wright is a brand stylist specializing in the critical components that forge resilient and compelling brands. Her expertise spans from fundamental elements—like business names, logos, tones, color schemes, websites, and visual aesthetics—to crafting engaging content, including standout branding photography, and compelling videos.

She leads a world-renowned team of creative artists: graphic designers, photographers, videographers, web designers, content strategists, and podcast producers who bring new ideas to life and elevate their clients' current efforts.

Her agency, Tally Creative, pioneers a groundbreaking "blitz" methodology for brand development. This approach compresses what would traditionally require a year-long engagement with an agency into an intensive, three-day immersive experience. This format is ideal for driven individuals juggling dual brands, such as authors, speakers, agents, and coaches, who often need to manage both a professional and a personal brand simultaneously.

In the constantly evolving world of branding, Juliet is not just a trailblazer; she's a visionary, an innovator, and a strategist, forever raising the bar on what's possible. With each project, she not only shapes brands but also the futures of the individuals behind them.

Connect:

Unlock the power of exceptional branding by collaborating with Juliet. From speaking engagements and podcast features to in-depth consultations, Juliet and her dynamic team bring expertise to every project.

For lifelong learners, educators, and group leaders: This book's insights are just the beginning. You can either embark on our accompanying course independently or integrate its rich content into your class or group setting, offering a comprehensive branding perspective. With the flexibility to study solo or foster collaborative learning, our course adapts to meet your needs. Together, let's elevate the branding narrative for personal growth or collective enlightenment.

Connect with us at www.tallycreative.com or hello@tallycreative.com for the next chapter in your brand or educational journey.

Made in the USA
Las Vegas, NV
22 November 2023

81317128R00056